Birds
to Color

Illustrated by Jenny Cooper

Designed by Nelupa Hussain
Written by Megan Cullis

Keel-billed toucan

Golden-breasted starling

Also known as glossy starlings, these birds have shiny-looking feathers that glow bright colors in the sun.

In some lights they look black, making it difficult for their enemies to spot them.

Violet-blue wings

Metallic green head

Glossy starlings live in small flocks in the grasslands of Africa.

Using their sharp beaks, they poke at insect nests on the ground, looking for ants and termites to eat.

Lesser bird-of-paradise

These spectacular birds live in the rainforests of New Guinea.

Glossy green neck and throat

Male birds-of-paradise have long, showy tail feathers. They gather in groups to display their impressive tails to the females.

During the displays, the males fan out their tails and sing loudly.

Bird-of-paradise skins and feathers were brought to Europe in the 16th century, and sold to make hats.

During the Middle Ages, the birds were named 'birds-of-paradise' because people believed they floated in paradise until they died and fell to Earth.

Lesser flamingo

Lesser flamingos live in Africa and Southern Asia, near salty lakes or coastlines.

They eat shrimp and algae from the water, by sucking them up with their beaks.

Young flamingos are pale brown.

Chemicals in their food turn flamingos' feathers pink.

Sometimes, flamingos gather in huge groups, or flocks. Some flocks contain up to a million flamingos.

Long legs allow them to wade in deep water.

Webbed feet stop them sinking into the sand.

Scarlet macaws

Scarlet macaws are a type of parrot. They live in the tropical rainforests of Central and South America.

Their strong, curved beaks can crack into the shells of nuts and seeds.

Flying among the tree tops, their dazzling colors blend in with the dappled sunlight and bright flowers. This keeps them hidden from enemies.

In the Amazon rainforest, hundreds of macaws flock to clay riverbanks. They eat the clay to get minerals from it.

Macaws are sometimes kept as pets. They can be very noisy, and are good at copying human voices.

Gouldian finch

Gouldian finches have red, black or yellow heads. Their bodies are splashed with green, yellow, purple and red.

They live in the tropical grasslands of Australia.

Males

Females have paler feathers, with pinkish purple chests.

Female

Gouldian finches often make their nests in the hollows of trees.

Greater double-collared sunbird

These small birds are found in shrubland, parks and gardens in South Africa. They eat nectar, fruit and bugs.

When feeding on nectar, they use their long, curved beaks to poke inside flowers.

Aloe flower

They have thin, hairy tongues to suck up nectar.

The males have striking red and blue bands across their chests, and metallic green heads.

The females are brown, with yellowish brown bellies.

Sometimes, greater double-collared sunbirds hover in front of spiders' webs and pluck spiders to eat.

Keel-billed toucan

Sometimes known as 'rainbow-billed toucans', these striking birds live in the tropical rainforests of Latin America.

Even their enormous beaks are splashed with color. They use them to pick fruit from trees.

Their colorful feathers and beaks blend in with the dappled light of the rainforest. This keeps them safe from enemies.

Coffee berries

Toucans can't fly very well, so they hop from branch to branch.

Green-headed tanager

Green-headed tanagers live in rainforests, orchards and parks in South America.

As they flit through the trees, they flash their blue and green feathers.

They blend in well with their leafy surroundings, helping them to hide from danger.

Orange back

These are male tanagers. They have much brighter feathers than the females.

Hopping from branch to branch, tanagers search for small insects or fruit to eat.

Rainbow lorikeet

Rainbow lorikeets live in the tropical rainforests and woodlands of Australia, Indonesia and Papua New Guinea.

Their vibrant blue, green, yellow and red feathers help them to stay hidden among brightly colored tropical plants.

They use their sharp beaks to tear fruit apart, such as papaya, mangos and figs.

Umbrella tree fruit

Common kingfisher

Common kingfishers live by rivers and streams in Europe, Asia and North Africa.

This kingfisher is perching above the water, waiting for small fish to swim by.

When it spots a fish, it plunges into the water and snaps it up with its knife-shaped beak.

These are male kingfishers.

Kingfishers have an extra set of eyelids that are see-through. The eyelids protect the birds' eyes underwater.

A kingfisher's electric blue feathers flash green in the sun.

Blue tit

These common garden birds are found all over Europe.

Male blue tits have golden yellow bellies, which become more yellow the more caterpillars they eat.

Males

The females are paler.

They live in noisy flocks, calling to each other with a 'tsee-tsee-tsee' sound.

Blue tits also eat seeds, nuts and small insects.

Golden pheasant

Golden pheasants live wild in the mountain forests of China. Many are also kept in zoos in other parts of the world.

Long, striped tail feathers

Golden neck feathers

Males, like this one, have splendid red, gold and blue feathers, which they use to impress female pheasants.

Although they can fly, golden pheasants spend most of the time on the ground, looking for insects and grain to eat.

Lilac-breasted roller

Rollers are acrobatic birds, named because of the swoops, dives and 'rolls' they do in the air.

They live in the dry, open grasslands of Eastern Africa.

Forked tail----

The males and females both have electric blue, green and lilac feathers that are easy to spot, and warn other animals away.

Swooping through the air, they grab insects, lizards and small animals to eat.

Bee-eater

Bee-eaters live near riverbanks in
Europe, Africa and Asia. They eat
bees, wasps and other flying insects.

During the day, a bee-eater
perches on a branch waiting
for an insect to fly past...

...then it swoops
down and snatches
the insect in its beak.

Bee-eaters build their
nests in sandy banks,
digging holes in the earth
with their sharp beaks.

Their bronze and gold head
feathers blend in with their
sandy surroundings and keep
them hidden from enemies.

Mandarin ducks

Mandarin ducks are originally from Japan, China and Russia, but many now live in Western Europe.

Male mandarin ducks, like this one, have spiky red whiskers and orange tail feathers. Their colorful feathers attract females.

Orange tail feathers, called 'sails'

Female mandarin ducks are mostly brown with lighter patches.

In Japan, a pair of mandarin ducks is sometimes given as a wedding gift. They are said to symbolize a happy marriage.

Coloring hints and tips

You can use colored pencils, felt-tip markers, or watercolor paints or pencils to color in your pictures. If you use watercolors, put a piece of cardstock under your page to stop the rest of the book from getting wet.

Colored pencils

Colored pencils can give all kinds of different effects and are good for doing shading.

To fill in large areas, do lots of lines all going in the same direction.

In areas with shading, press firmly for the dark areas, then gradually reduce the pressure where the color gets lighter.

You can blend different colors together by shading them on top of each other.

Shading in dark areas

When you're coloring in, you'll find some areas covered with faint dots. These show you where to fill in with black.

Watercolors

Make watercolors lighter by adding more water, or darker by adding less.

Wet watercolors blur together.

For distinct colors, let one color dry before you add the next.

With thanks to Rob Hume and Katie Lovell
Digital manipulation by Nick Wakeford

First published in 2012 by Usborne Publishing Ltd, Usborne House, 83-85 Saffron Hill, London EC1N 8RT, England. www.usborne.com